FOUR JOURNEYS

Created by
Julia Rudakova

Illustrated by
Erika Maccarinelli

Breathing retraining exercises for children.
Breathe for calm, focus, active play and sweet dreams.

Four Journeys © Julia Rudakova 2021

www.oxygenrevolution.com.au/four-journeys

First published in Australia in 2021
Text © Julia Rudakova
Illustrations © Erika Maccarinelli

ISBN: 978-0-6453193-0-9
Printed in Australia

Dedicated to Kostya and Leon, my sons
and best teachers on this life journey.

WHERE TO?

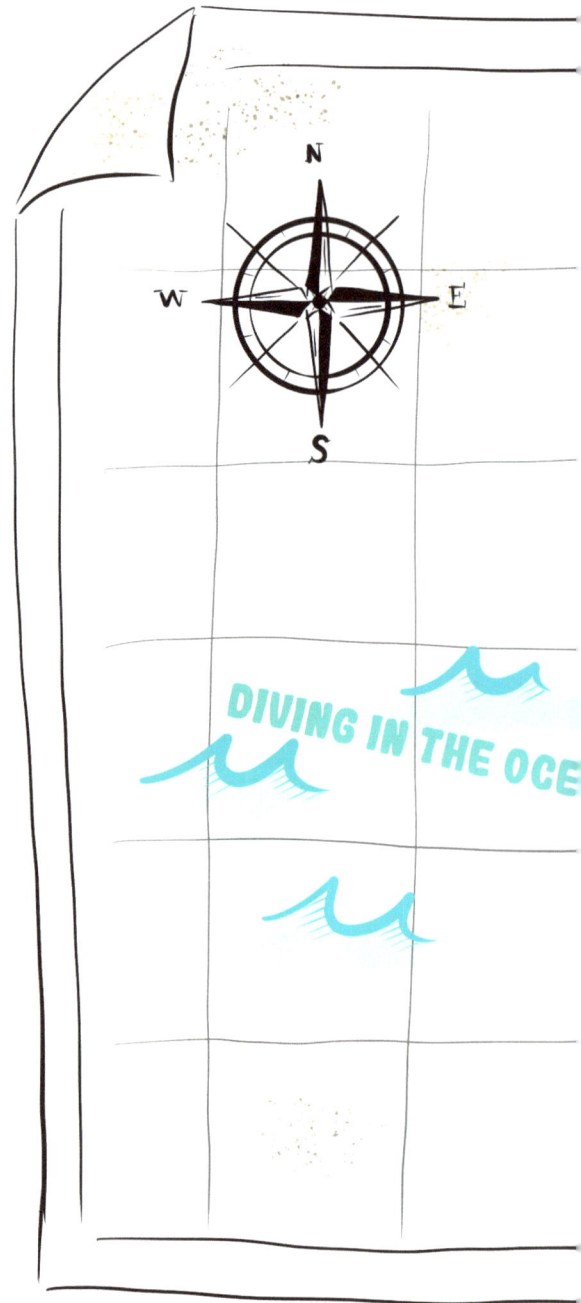

DIVING IN THE OCE

HOT AIR BALLOON TRIP

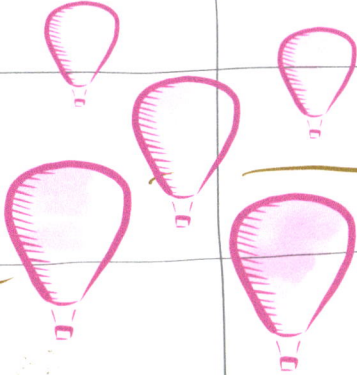

MOUNTAIN ADVENTURE

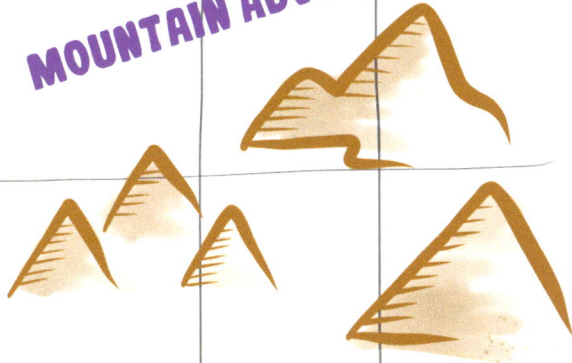

WHITE WATER RAFTING
ADVENTURE

FOR PARENTS

This book was created to help your children re-establish nasal breathing, be calmer and have better sleep. In my clinical practice and through personal experience, I have observed hundreds of children with dysfunctional patterns of breathing – through the mouth. It is well researched that mouth breathing contributes to craniofacial bone malformation, malocclusions (crooked teeth), dental decay and gum disease, aggravation of asthma and other respiratory conditions, poor sleep and behavioural issues. Of course, all of the health problems listed above are multi-faceted and must be approached in a holistic way.

It must be noted that behind mouth breathing may lie various types of allergies or a deviated septum, for instance. Those underlying causes may require naturopathic, surgical or other interventions. But correcting dysfunctional breathing patterns should always be addressed. On the opposite side of dysfunctional breathing is gentle, slow, nasal breathing, which is conducive to restful sleep, mental focus, correct craniofacial formation, decreased anxiety, improved mood, reduced respiratory symptoms, better digestion and lowered incidence of dental diseases.

Breath is something we take for granted; it is automatic but, at the same time, we can control it. If you notice that your child (or you) breathes through the mouth at times, that you can hear your child breathe when they sit next to you; if you notice that their breathing is laboured, audible, rapid, with chest moving up and down rather than the stomach inflating and deflating (diaphragmatic breathing), then it is time to intervene.

This book is an excellent tool to work on re-establishing good breathing habits – through visualisation and engaging fine motor skills.

Focusing on breathing is also a form of mindfulness. It brings us back in the present moment, reduces anxiety and creates calmness through lowering our heart rate.

I hope you enjoy journeying through four different landscapes and practicing breath work and mindfulness.

HOW TO USE THIS BOOK

While travelling through four different landscapes, use the colourful illustrations, read the instructions to your child and join in the adventure yourself! You can choose a favourite landscape and do that adventure every day. With practice, you might try doing it without the book. You may also need to explain, in simple terms, why it is important to train ourselves back to nasal breathing. Tell your child, that when they were born, they were breathing only through the nose and sometimes allergies make us mouth breathe and it is important to retrain our bodies back to nose breathing to have ...... (put what is more important to you and your child here – good sleep, straight, beautiful and healthy teeth, good mood, a happy day at the kindergarten, etc.). You may want to tell them that our nose warms, moistens and filters the air for the lungs. And when breathing through the mouth, the air that goes into the lungs is cold, dry and unfiltered – the dust particles go straight into the lungs, which may make us cough.

Some basic rules for working with this book.

All exercises/adventures are done with mouth closed and lips together, using only the nose for breathing. The most beneficial way to do them is to repeat an adventure a few times in a row. Do the exercises every day.

Some exercises require breath holding to retrain the receptors in the brain for the optimal carbon dioxide and oxygen levels in the blood (read more on blood chemistry and breathing on my website – the link is on the "Resources" page at the end of the book). You might want to practice breath holds with your child prior to going on the Whitewater Rafting adventures in this book. The Mountain and Hot-Air balloon adventures don't require this skill, so it is safe to start with those.

I also recorded an audio visualisation for children. The link to the audio is in the "Resources" section at the end of this book. The visualisation is particularly useful to do before sleep, while lying in bed. Feel free to change the wording and transform it into your magical bedtime routine with your child or use it as is.

LEGEND

1 2 3 4   Pink numbers means inhale/breathe in.

1 2 3 4   Red numbers means hold your breath.

1 2 3 4   Blue numbers means exhale/breathe out.

AN OVERVIEW OF 4 JOURNEYS:
UNDERSTAND THE BOOK BETTER

The book is interactive; it encourages your child to use their fine motor skills and trace pictures in the book, engaging them not only visually, but kinaesthetically as well.

MOUNTAIN ADVENTURE

Mountain adventure is a basic breathing exercise. We breathe in to the count of four, stop for 1 second and breathe out to the count of four. This exercise is a fantastic start for any child or adult who has been mouth breathing for a prolonged period of time. The receptors in the respiratory centre of the brain will be happy with this gradual breathing retraining, where the only thing we change is switching to nasal breathing with a slight reduction of breathing rate.

Engage kinaesthetic experience and use fine motor skills to trace the outline of the mountain up to the top on the inhalation, stop there to "look at the view" for one second, then trace the mountain slope down on the exhalation while counting. No breath holding at this stage. A one-second stop is a natural pause between breathing in and out. You may choose not to draw attention to it at all.

Tip: Try doing the exercise yourself first before introducing it to your child. Once you have tried it together a couple of times, encourage (and attempt yourself as well) to breathe slower (count slower).

WHITE WATER RAFTING ADVENTURE

This exercise introduces breath holds. Please, practice them with your child beforehand. If your child has taken swimming lessons, they would already know how to do it.
When you go down the river on the raft, inhale to the count of four, then with a wave over the raft, hold the breath to the count of four, once out of the wave, move farther down the river while exhaling to the count of four and, with the second wave coming on, hold your breath again to the count of four.

Repeat. This is a "four by four" breathing exercise. It encourages the accumulation of nitric oxide in the nasal cavity, which is antimicrobial (great to do during the winter season!), it also helps clear the nasal passages to breathe easier. It slows down the breathing and encourages relaxation.

HOT AIR BALLOON TRIP

This is a relaxation exercise.
Hot Air balloon is a very slow-breathing exercise. Breathe in to the count of 6 when going up on the colourful hot air balloon, then breathe out to the count of 6 when descending to the ground. Ask the child to trace the trajectory of the balloon, counting out loud for them. Remind them to breathe only through the nose and keep lips together at all times.

DIVING IN THE OCEAN

This is a breath-holding exercise. Breath holds are a crucial part of breathing retraining. They help correct the levels of carbon dioxide in the blood, oxygenating the cells in the body better.
Read more about the Bohr effect on www.oxygenrevolution.com.au/breath-holds

The illustration and the narration of a beautiful warm day promote relaxation before holding the breath. It is important to do breath holding after EXHALING. Breathe in, breathe out, pinch your nose (this is an important step), dive from the boat into the warm water. When you can't hold your breath any more, release the nose pinch and start breathing through the NOSE. Go back to the boat, rest for a few breaths, then "dive in" again.

Note for all exercises: for a child who has been mouth breathing for a while, it is recommended to use a Micropore© tape or a Myotape© (both available from www.oxygenrevolution.com) as a reminder to use the nose, not the mouth, for breathing.

MOUNTAIN ADVENTURE

What a magnificent mountain range! Look at the snowy peaks!

You are going to climb up and down the mountains. Trace the mountain outline with your finger as you go.

On your way to the mountain top, breathe in while counting to 4.

At the snowy peak stop for 1 second (hold your breath) – the views are truly amazing!!!

Now, slowly walk down and start breathing out, while counting to 4 again.

How many mountains can you climb today?
Set your timer to 2 minutes or 5 minutes and GO!

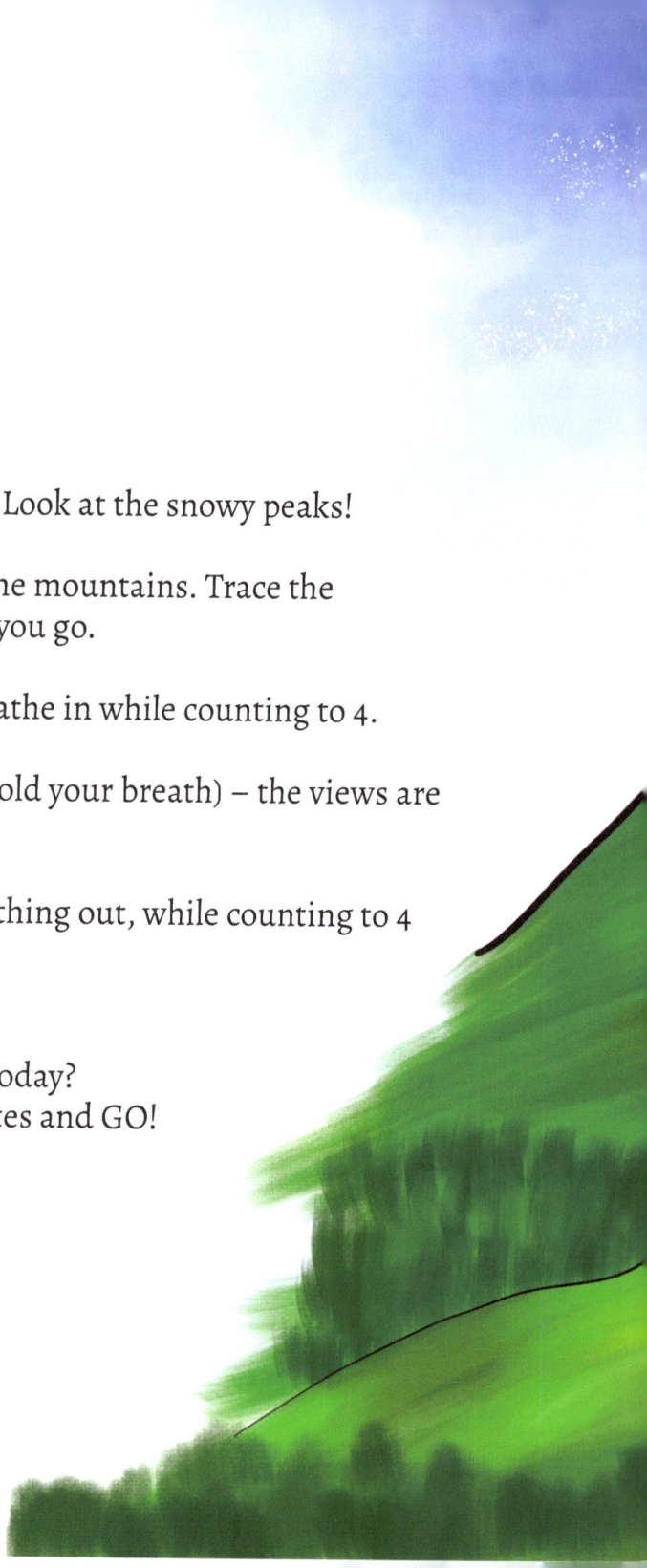

WHITE WATER RAFTING ADVENTURE

The river is fast and the water is cold.

Your challenge is to move through the waves and stay in the boat.
Hold on to your raft! You can do it!

Start at the highest point of the mountain river. Breathe in (1-2-3-4).
Ouch, icy water washes over your raft, hold your breath (1-2-3-4). Your
raft is out of the wave, breathe out (1-2-3-4). Look, another wave – hold
your breath (1-2-3-4)! And breathe in (1-2-3-4). A wave is over you –
hold your breath (1-2-3-4). And it's gone - breathe out (1-2-3-4). Watch
out,
another wave - hold your breath (1-2-3-4)!

Start all over again!

Set your timer for 2 or 5 minutes.

1234

1234

HOT AIR BALLOON TRIP

It is sunrise and there are a lot of colourful hot air balloons in the sky.

What an unforgettable experience it is to get to fly in one of them! Are you ready? The hot air balloon is very slow to go up in the sky and just as slow to come down back to the ground.

Set your timer to 2 minutes and trace the path of the hot air balloon going up while breathing in (1-2-3-4-5-6) and trace it back to the ground while breathing out (1-2-3-4-5-6).
Repeat.

1
2
3
4
5
6

DIVING IN THE OCEAN

It is a beautiful day in tropical Queensland, Australia. The turquoise water is warm and the sunshine reflects off its surface.

Dip your toes in the water, feel its pleasant warmth. Right here, on the beach, halfway in water, halfway on the sand, you can see a boat with a transparent bottom. Get in and row away from the shore to the best spot to dive. Watch the colourful tropical fish swimming underneath. This is a perfect spot!
Stand up in the boat, breathe in, breathe out, pinch your nose and dive into the warm turquoise water. When you can't hold your breath any more, go up to the boat and breathe through your nose for a bit before you dive back in.

Set a timer and go diving for 2-3 minutes.

RESOURCES

1. Information about the dangers of mouth breathing and the benefits of nasal breathing:

www.oxygenrevolution.com.au/mouth-breathing-blood-chemistry

2. Learn about health benefits of breath holds:

www.oxygenrevolution.com.au/breath-holds

3. An audio recording "A Journey to the heart of the Universe", a relaxation visualisation for children and adults:

www.oxygenrevolution.com.au/childrens-visualisation

4. Video demonstration on how to use the book "Four Journeys" with children:

www.oxygenrevolution.com.au/four-journeys

ABOUT THE AUTHOR: MEET JULIA

Julia Rudakova is a naturopath who specialises in respiratory conditions and has been running the functional breathing program for adults and children online and at her clinic in Melbourne, Australia. Her passion to use breath work as the first step to healing stems from her personal health journey as well as her extensive research into respiratory health and into the link between breathing and mental and emotional health.

Julia loves creative work, and this book is a product of love and deep desire to help families feel empowered and in control of their health.

ABOUT THE ILLUSTRATOR: MEET ERIKA

Erika Maccarinelli is a designer with a bachelor degree in industrial design from Politecnico di Milano, Italy and RMIT University, Melbourne. She started illustrating books for children while teaching Italian to non-native speakers as a way to better interact with her little students and create more memorable, inspiring and enjoyable classes.

She is based in the beautiful Dandenong Ranges, in Victoria, where she lives with her husband and her dog. She is also an avid gardener and a sustainable living enthusiast.

www.ingramcontent.com/pod-product-compliance
Lightning Source LLC
Chambersburg PA
CBHW042026090426
42811CB00016B/1757

* 9 7 8 0 6 4 5 3 1 9 3 0 9 *